Financial well-being: The goal of financial education

Consumer Financial Protection Bureau

January 2015

Table of contents

Executive summary

Consumers of financial products and services need both a safe, transparent marketplace, and the financial capability to navigate that marketplace effectively. The Consumer Financial Protection Bureau (CFPB) addresses the first aspect through its supervision, enforcement, rulemaking, and other functions. Helping consumers acquire financial capability is also an integral part of the CFPB's consumer financial protection mission, as reflected in numerous provisions of the Dodd-Frank Wall Street Reform and Consumer Protection Act of 2010. The Act charges the Bureau with researching, developing, promoting, and implementing financial literacy programs and activities.[1]

In this report we describe our initial research – conducted with a team of expert researchers[2] – into how people acquire financial capability, which we undertook specifically to inform financial education and improve consumer outcomes. Our overarching objective is to determine how to define and measure the success of different financial literacy strategies so that we have a basis for measuring different strategies' effectiveness. And for this, we need to define the end goal of financial education.

A growing consensus is emerging that the ultimate measure of success for financial literacy efforts should be improvement in individual financial well-being. But financial well-being has

---

[1] An important financial literacy mandate is set forth in Section 1013(d) of the Dodd-Frank Act, which directs the Bureau, through its Office of Financial Education, to develop and implement initiatives intended to "educate and empower consumers to make better informed financial decisions" and to "develop and implement a strategy to improve the financial literacy of consumers." (12 U.S.C. § 5493(d)(1)&(2)). The Dodd-Frank Act also mandated the creation of other offices within the Bureau that are responsible for, among other things, developing financial education and policy initiatives to support the financial well-being of particular segments of the consumer population (12 U.S.C. § 5493(b),(e),(g)).

[2] The research team responsible for conducting the research and analysis described in this report includes Bureau staff as well as a team of research contractors led by the Corporation for Enterprise Development (CFED), including the University of Wisconsin-Madison Center for Financial Security, the Urban Institute, ICF International, and Vector Psychometrics.

never been explicitly defined, nor is there a standard way to measure it. Overall, the literature paints a picture of nuanced, complex interactions between financial knowledge, understanding, and actions taken. However, rigorously identified links between these factors and financial outcomes have yet to be established.

Our project provides a conceptual framework for defining and measuring success in financial education by delivering a proposed definition of financial well-being, and insight into the factors that contribute to it. This framework is grounded in the existing literature, expert opinion, and the experiences and voice of the consumer garnered through in-depth, one-on-one interviews with working-age and older consumers.

Financial well-being

The definition of financial well-being that we propose is based on the consumer perspective revealed by the nearly 60 hours of open-ended interviews our research team conducted. Our research suggests financial well-being can be defined as a state of being wherein you:

- Have control over day-to-day, month-to-month finances;

- Have the capacity to absorb a financial shock;

- Are on track to meet your financial goals; and

- Have the financial freedom to make the choices that allow you to enjoy life.

Because individuals value different things, traditional measures such as income or net worth, while important, do not necessarily or fully capture this last aspect of financial well-being.

We then sought to identify the specific types of knowledge, behavior, and personal traits that help people achieve greater financial well-being. Our research focused on those personal drivers of well-being that may be influenced by financial education and other decision-making supports. Of course many factors beyond an individual's control play a significant role in financial outcomes, but our research asks, "Given people's current financial circumstances, how can they make the best of their situation?"

The hypotheses we propose about key drivers of financial well-being were developed by synthesizing three methodologies in this project—literature reviews, consumer and financial practitioner interviews, and ongoing and iterative consultation with an expert panel. The hypotheses fall into three categories: *financial behaviors*, *financial knowledge*, and *personal traits*.

Financial behaviors

Four types of behaviors are hypothesized to support financial well-being:

- Effective routine money management, which encompasses often unconscious habits, intuitions, and decision-making shortcuts (heuristics);

- Financial research and knowledge-seeking, which support purposeful, informed financial decision-making;

- Financial planning and goal-setting, which give purpose and structure to individual financial decisions; and

- Following through on financial decisions, the final step between intentions and desired outcomes.

In other words, our research suggests that people have higher levels of financial well-being when they Ask, Plan, and Act, coupled with a strong habit or tendency to live within their means in terms of their day-to-day financial choices.

Financial knowledge

In both published research and our interviewees' responses, we found that the link between knowledge and behavior is always affected by individual characteristics like personality, attitudes, and non-cognitive skills, and by context. Our primary hypothesis about the type of knowledge that supports financial well-being is a set of skills we call "financial ability," which encompasses:

- Knowing when and how to find reliable information to make a financial decision;

- Knowing how to process financial information to make sound financial decisions; and

- Knowing how to execute financial decisions, adapting as necessary to stay on track.

A growing consensus points toward this notion of financial ability: that in addition to a knowledge component, financial literacy has an action component—that is, the ability or skills to put financial knowledge to use.

Personal traits

Personal attitudes and beliefs, non-cognitive skills, and personality traits all influence financial behavior and play a role in mediating the connection between knowledge and behavior. Based on our research, we hypothesize that the following four types of personal traits are likely to affect financial well-being through their influence on behavior and/or preferences and expectations:

- Comparing yourself to your own standards, not to others (internal frame of reference);

- Being highly motived to stay on track in the face of obstacles (perseverance);

- Having a tendency to plan for the future, control impulses, and think creatively to address unexpected challenges (executive functioning); and

- Believing in your ability to influence your financial outcomes (financial self-efficacy).

Discussion

Taken together, this set of hypotheses suggests how particular behaviors, skills, and traits appear to support or predict financial well-being, given a certain level of opportunity. This suggests fascinating possibilities for meaningful research into approaches that could powerfully enable individuals to achieve and maintain financial well-being.

The CFPB seeks to use this research to engage with the financial education field toward collectively establishing a set of best practices in financial literacy and capability that are grounded in evidence-based research and able to make a difference in consumers' lives. Using the findings of the research reported here, the CFPB is committed to furthering its consumer financial literacy mission through fostering approaches grounded in an understanding of financial well-being as a key measure of effective financial education. This work presents a unique opportunity to move consumer financial capability practices forward.

1. Introduction

An essential part of the mission of the Consumer Financial Protection Bureau (CFPB or Bureau) is empowering consumers to take control over their financial lives. In addition to needing a safe, transparent marketplace, which we address through our supervision, enforcement, rulemaking, and other functions, consumers need the financial capability[3] to navigate that marketplace effectively to serve their own life goals. This aspect of our mission is reflected in numerous provisions of the Dodd-Frank Wall Street Reform and Consumer Protection Act of 2010 (Dodd-Frank Act) that charge the Bureau with researching, developing, promoting, and implementing financial literacy programs and activities.[4]

Fulfilling this aspect of our mission requires that we know what approaches are effective in promoting financial literacy and capability. According to a 2011 Government Accountability Office (GAO) report on financial literacy, "[r]elatively few evidence-based evaluations of financial literacy programs have been conducted, limiting what is known about which specific methods and strategies are most effective."[5] The CFPB is taking up this challenge to provide stronger evidence of what works, in order to support and guide efforts to improve the

---

[3] The charter establishing the President's Advisory Council on Financial Capability defines financial capability as "the capacity, based on knowledge, skills and access, to manage financial resources effectively." See http://www.treasury.gov/resource-center/financial-education/Documents/PACFC%202010%20Amended%20Charter.pdf (2010) (accessed October 13, 2014).

[4] An important financial literacy mandate is set forth in Section 1013(d) of the Dodd-Frank Act, which directs the Bureau, through its Office of Financial Education, to develop and implement initiatives intended to "educate and empower consumers to make better informed financial decisions" and to "develop and implement a strategy to improve the financial literacy of consumers . . . consistent with the National Strategy for Financial Literacy . . .." (12 U.S.C. § 5493(d)(1)&(2)). The Dodd-Frank Act also mandated the creation of other offices within the Bureau that are responsible for, among other things, developing financial education and policy initiatives to support the financial well-being of particular segments of the consumer population (12 U.S.C. § 5493(b),(e),(g)).

[5] U.S. Government Accountability Office. "Financial Literacy: A Federal Certification Process for Providers Would Pose Challenges." GAO-11-614. http://www.gao.gov/assets/330/320214.pdf (2011) (accessed October 13, 2014).

effectiveness and quality of financial education, and therefore improve consumers' financial decision making to achieve their life goals.[6]

A foundational step is a well-grounded way to define success for financial literacy initiatives. Reaching the goal of consumers making better informed decisions requires identifying educational and informational strategies that can change consumer behavior in the marketplace in ways that help them achieve their life goals—not merely improve their knowledge of financial facts in a classroom. A major task for the CFPB is therefore determining how to define and measure the success of different financial literacy strategies in a way that corresponds with our ultimate objective of helping consumers to effectively manage their financial lives in ways that move them toward their life goals.

A growing consensus is emerging that the ultimate measure of success for financial literacy efforts should be individual financial well-being. The vision for the U.S. National Strategy for Financial Literacy is "[s]ustained financial well-being for U.S. individuals and families."[7] This vision is consistent with that of the OECD[8]'s International Network on Financial Education (INFE), in which the CFPB participates, which describes the ultimate goal of financial literacy as "individual financial well-being."[9] However, this concept has not been explicitly defined, nor does a standard way to measure it exist in the financial literacy field. Significant and ongoing efforts have been

> **The ultimate measure of success for financial literacy efforts should be individual financial well-being.**

---

[6] The CFPB's financial literacy and capability research work is described broadly in Section 4 of the CFPB's 2014 "Financial Literacy Annual Report." Available at http://www.consumerfinance.gov/reports/financial-literacy-annual-report-2014/ (2014) (accessed October 13, 2014).

[7] See Financial Literacy and Education Commission, "Promoting Financial Success in the United States: National Strategy for Financial Literacy." Available at http://www.treasury.gov/resource-center/financial-education/Documents/NationalStrategyBook_12310%20(2).pdf (2011) (accessed October 13, 2014): p. 7.

[8] The Organization for Economic Cooperation and Development (OECD) is a unique forum where the governments of 34 democracies with market economies work with each other, as well as with more than 70 non-member economies to promote economic growth, prosperity, and sustainable development. To learn more, see http://usoecd.usmission.gov/mission/overview.html.

[9] See OECD INFE, "Measuring Financial Literacy: Questionnaire and Guidance Notes for Conducting an Internationally Comparable Survey of Financial Literacy." Paris: OECD. Available at http://www.oecd.org/finance/financial-education/49319977.pdf (2011) (accessed October 13, 2014): p. 3.

undertaken to understand and measure financial literacy and capability[10], but not the state of being that is meant to result from high levels of financial literacy and capability.

Accordingly, the Bureau has undertaken a rigorous set of research activities[11] to understand and formally define financial well-being—for the first time—in ways that allow it to be measured and that allow meaningful comparisons between approaches to achieving it. Our goal was a definition that could gain widespread acceptance across varied relevant professions and disciplines; could be effective across a range of different economic, geographic, life-stage, and other contexts; and would not need to change over time.

In addition, we sought to identify the specific types of knowledge, behavior, and personal traits that help some people navigate the financial ups and downs of life particularly effectively. This is an important area of inquiry because it not only helps us identify which financial-capability tools, habits and skills may be helpful for consumers to acquire, but it also reveals which intermediate outcome measures we can rely on for measuring the success of financial capability initiatives—that is, which intermediate outcomes tend to precede real improvement in individual financial well-being.

This research focuses on the areas where the CFPB's and others' financial capability efforts can most effectively help to empower consumers—on those personal drivers of well-being that may be influenced by financial education and other decision-making supports. While factors beyond an individual's control, such as structural opportunities, macro-economic context, and family resources, of course play a significant role in financial outcomes, our research focuses on a complementary question: Given people's current financial circumstances, how can people make the best of their situation?

_____

[10] See, for example: The World Bank (2013). "Making Sense of Financial Capability Surveys around the World: A Review of Existing Financial Capability and Literacy Measurement Instruments." Available at http://responsiblefinance.worldbank.org/~/media/GIAWB/FL/Documents/Misc/Financial-Capability-Review.pdf. (accessed October 13, 2014)
FINRA Investor Education Foundation (2013). "Financial Capability in the United States: Report of Findings from the 2012 National Financial Capability Study." Available at http://usfinancialcapability.org/ and,
OECD. _PISA 2012 Results: Students and Money: Financial Literacy Skills for the 21st Century (Volume VI)_. PISA, OECD Publishing. http://www.oecd.org/pisa/keyfindings/PISA-2012-results-volume-vi.pdf (2014) (accessed October 13, 2014).
[11] The research team responsible for conducting the research and analysis described in this report includes Bureau staff as well as a team of research contractors led by the Corporation for Enterprise Development (CFED), including the University of Wisconsin-Madison Center for Financial Security, the Urban Institute, ICF International, and Vector Psychometrics.

We seek to lay the groundwork for further empowering consumers to take control of their financial lives. Our work to do so includes recognizing financial well-being as the ultimate goal of financial education; helping to establish a common understanding of what constitutes financial well-being; examining what specific types of knowledge, skills, behavior, and personal attributes tend to help one achieve greater financial well-being; and developing rigorous tools to measure outcomes related to achieving financial well-being. This paper reports on the design, findings, and implications of this research to date.

2. Research design and methods

This research on financial well-being follows directly from, and is intended to inform, the CFPB's larger consumer financial literacy mandate. We have started by studying working-age and older consumers to learn about financial well-being as they understand it. What financial outcomes have they achieved, and what do they believe led to those outcomes? From that vantage point, we hope to be able—in a later stage of research—to identify approaches we can employ with youth that will affect their financial outcomes later in life.

The key topics this project explores are:

- What is financial well-being?

- What behaviors (given a certain level of opportunity) lead to greater financial well-being?

- What knowledge, abilities, attitudes, and traits lead to these behaviors?

- How do social and economic contexts influence these personal factors?

To ensure that the factors we identify pertain broadly to consumers in America across life stage, we examine whether and how the above may differ between working-age and older consumers. Studying older consumers also offers the benefit of learning how older consumers view their working-age life stage in hindsight.

2.1   Literature-based research

To gain expertise in the state of current research, we reviewed more than 150 articles from a dozen fields.[12] We targeted topics of particular relevance, which can be expressed as a series of questions:

- What is understood (and what is agreed among experts) about what financial well-being is, what behaviors lead to it, and what knowledge and skills and attitudes support those behaviors?

- How does financial knowledge translate into financial behavior?

- What can we learn about how knowledge translates into behavior generally, from research in areas other than household finance?

- Do particular classes of knowledge translate into behavior differently or more effectively than others—and if so, how should we classify different aspects of financial knowledge to best help us examine such dynamics?

There exists a rich literature to draw from, but interpreting its implications can be a challenge, especially regarding ultimate outcomes such as financial well-being. For example, explicit knowledge of financial concepts such as inflation or the time value of money or compound interest have all been shown to be correlated with better financial decisions in multiple studies.[13] In contrast, several studies have shown that exposure to financial education (i.e., the dissemination of just such knowledge) does not necessarily lead to improved financial knowledge after the fact,[14] although financial education that closely precedes a financial decision

---

[12] These include Consumer Finance, Economics, Behavioral Economics, Psychology (cognitive and developmental), Health, Education, Philosophy, Conservation, Environmental Science, Sociology and Marketing.
[13] Gerardi, Kristopher, Lorenz Goette, and Stephan Meier. "Financial literacy and subprime mortgage delinquency: Evidence from a survey matched to administrative data." Federal Reserve of Atlanta.
https://www.frbatlanta.org/research/pubs/wp/working_paper_2010-10.aspx (2010) (accessed October 9th, 2014).
Hung, Angela A., Andrew M. Parker, and Joanne K. Yoong. "Defining and Measuring Financial Literacy." RAND Corporation. http://www.rand.org/content/dam/rand/pubs/working_papers/2009/RAND_WR708.pdf (2009) (accessed October 9th, 2014).
Lusardi, Annamaria, and Olivia S. Mitchell. "How ordinary consumers make complex economic decisions: Financial literacy and retirement readiness." http://www.nber.org/papers/w15350.pdf (2009) (accessed October 9th, 2014).
[14] Fernandes, Daniel, John G. Lynch, Jr., and Richard G. Netemeyer. "Financial Literacy, Financial Education, and Downstream Financial Behaviors." *Management Science.* 60(8) (2014): 1861–1883.

has more impact on behavior than education which is more remote from the behavior it seeks to support[15], and adding years of general education—particularly college education—does correlate with improved financial knowledge.[16] Still other research suggests that financial training based on rules of thumb (i.e. heuristics[17]) can lead to greater improvement in financial behavior than does training that focuses on formal financial concepts.[18]

> **Relatively little has been published on a causal relationship between financial knowledge and financial behavior.**

Most research into individuals' financial knowledge, education, and behavior has been published in the field of household finance, but relatively little has been published on a causal relationship between financial knowledge and financial behavior. Therefore, we began by casting a wide net to garner more general insights into the relationship between knowledge and behavior and the factors that mediate that relationship. The range of fields studied included health, health counseling, energy consumption, education, cognitive psychology, sociology, and social marketing. In none of the fields we surveyed, however, has the relationship between knowledge and behavior been fully determined and explained.

Moreover, the field of household finance lacks generally accepted definitions and measurements of financial knowledge, financial well-being, and financial behavior. With rare exceptions, financial knowledge has typically been defined only in terms of factual knowledge of specific financial concepts or as specific levels of numeracy. Only a handful of studies have looked at how different types of financial knowledge influence financial behavior or what circumstances either limit or catalyze the translation of financial knowledge into behaviors conducive to financial well-being. Overall, we found understanding of financial well-being to be very limited; often

---

Yates, Dan, and Chris Ward. "Financial literacy: Examining the knowledge transfer of personal finance from high school to college to adulthood." *American Journal of Business Education.* 4(1) (2011): 65–78.

Mandell, Lewis, and Linda Schmid Klein. "The Impact of Financial Literacy Education on Subsequent Financial Behavior." *Journal of Financial Counseling and Planning.* 20(1) (2009): 15–24.

[15] Fernandes, Daniel, John G. Lynch, Jr., and Richard G. Netemeyer. "Financial Literacy, Financial Education, and Downstream Financial Behaviors." *Management Science.* 60(8) (2014): 1861–1883.

[16] Yates, Dan, and Chris Ward. "Financial literacy: Examining the knowledge transfer of personal finance from high school to college to adulthood." *American Journal of Business Education.* 4(1) (2011): 65–78.

[17] Tversky, Amos, and Daniel Kahneman. "Judgment under uncertainty: Heuristics and biases." *Science.*185(4157) (1974): 1124–1131.

[18] Drexler, Alejandro, Greg Fischer, and Antoinette Schoar. "Keeping it simple: Financial literacy and rules of thumb." *American Economic Journal: Applied Economics.* 6(2) (2014): 1–31.

well-being is conflated with behaviors considered "positive" because they are presumed to lead one in the direction of financial well-being, but with little or no evidence from robust longitudinal studies. Nor has the relationship between attitudes and financial well-being been extensively studied,[19] although findings in health-related fields and elsewhere suggest that such links could be important.

Overall, our literature reviews revealed critical gaps in existing research from the perspective of the CFPB's specific need for broadly applicable, evidence-based measures through which to identify effective financial education approaches. Few studies in the field of household finance have combined large samples, long time spans, and control populations. In many cases, the relevant concepts have been loosely defined,[20] and the majority of studies have focused on correlation, rather than causation.[21] Results have seemed inconsistent, with different studies appearing to point in different directions. Our examination of the relevant literature—and published discussions[22] of the issues we encountered—underscored the need for widely agreed-upon definitions and measures of financial well-being and its key drivers as a necessary first step toward research into effective education strategies.

Our project attempts to address these issues by delivering a proposed definition of financial well-being, and insight into the personal factors that may contribute to it, which together provide a conceptual framework for further research to illuminate the bigger picture and identify the missing links. This framework is grounded in expert opinion, the existing literature, and—most importantly—the experiences and voice of the consumer.

---

[19] For examples of where it has been, see:
Lown, Jean M. "Development and validation of a financial self-efficacy scale." *Journal of Financial Counseling and Planning*. 22(2) (2012): 54–63.
Forbes, James, and S. Murat Kara. "Confidence mediates how investment knowledge influences investing self-efficacy." *Journal of Economic Psychology*. 31(3) (2010): 435-443.
[20] Huston, Sandra J. "Measuring financial literacy." *The Journal of Consumer Affairs*. 44(2) (2010): 296–316.
[21] Fernandes, Daniel, John G. Lynch, Jr., and Richard G. Netemeyer. "Financial Literacy, Financial Education, and Downstream Financial Behaviors." *Management Science*. 60(8) (2014): 1861–1883.
[22] Fernandes, Daniel, John G. Lynch, Jr., and Richard G. Netemeyer. "Financial Literacy, Financial Education, and Downstream Financial Behaviors." *Management Science*. 60(8) (2014): 1861–1883.
Hastings, Justine S., Brigitte C. Madrian, and William L. Skimmyhorn. 2013. "Financial literacy, financial education and economic outcomes." *Annual Review of Economics*. 5(1): 347–373.
Hung, Angela A., Erik Meijer, Kata Mihaly, Joanne K. Yoong. "Building Up, Spending Down: Financial Literacy, Retirement Savings Management, and Decumulation." RAND Corporation.
http://www.rand.org/content/dam/rand/pubs/working_papers/2009/RAND_WR712.pdf (2009) (accessed October 10th, 2014).

2.2 Qualitative research

Our qualitative research comprised in-depth, one-on-one interviews[23] conducted with 59 adult consumers[24] and an additional 30 financial practitioners—professionals who provide financial advice, education, services or products to consumers.[25] These one-hour interviews focused on how each person defined financial well-being for themselves (or their clients) and what factors they felt related to different levels of financial well-being based on their own personal experiences and the experiences of those around them. The research team transcribed and analyzed 1,600 pages of interview transcripts, from which responses were sorted, coded, and then catalogued using computer-aided qualitative data analysis software. This software helped us identify themes and understand how concepts related to one another and played out in the larger context of respondents' comments.

Our consumer interviewees—who will be referred to henceforth in this report as "consumers," were regionally and socio-demographically diverse, with interviews conducted in California, Georgia, Illinois, Tennessee, Washington, D.C., and Wyoming. There were somewhat more women than men, with persons from a full range of working age and older consumer age groups represented. Study participants were ethnically and racially diverse, had different marital and employment statuses, a wide range of incomes, and, within the older group, a variety of income sources. They had varied educational backgrounds, although persons with at least a college degree were over-represented relative to the U.S. adult population. The financial practitioners we interviewed—referred to in the rest of the report as "practitioners"—represented a range of professions and clientele characteristics, but also frequently spoke from their own experience as individuals.

---

[23] This information collection was approved by the Office of Management and Budget (OMB) under OMB No. 3170-0036.

[24] Forty-one of the consumers were between the ages of 18 and 61 and another 18 over the age of 61.

[25] Self-identified professions included: financial planner, elder lawyer, credit counselor, consumer loan officer, financial educator, financial advisor, social worker, financial coach, tax preparation adviser, and financial service professional.

2.3   Consultation with a panel of experts

The research team next shared both the findings of the project literature review and a summary of catalogued comments and themes extracted from the interview transcripts with a panel of a dozen leading academic and practitioner experts in the fields of consumer finance and financial capability. While the results of the qualitative research were already converging toward a common set of themes, collaborative discussion with the expert panel further elucidated the themes, and helped place them in the context of the broader existing literature. Ultimately, the research team and panel jointly distilled the results into a set of hypotheses about key drivers—that is, about the contributing influence of various personal attitudes, knowledge, and behaviors on financial well-being. Our research team then constructed a conceptual framework for understanding how these key drivers may relate to one another and to financial well-being. This framework is presented below, in the Discussion section.

The CFPB chose to frame the insights about what influences financial well-being as hypotheses, for two reasons: first, because many of the themes arose from the interviewees' own views about financial well-being and how it works—in a real sense, their own personal hypotheses—and second, to facilitate testing. Framing the results of this initial research as testable hypotheses will facilitate the design of future studies to help identify which hypotheses can be shown to be valid, which are most important, and which are perhaps less relevant.

3. Defining financial well-being

3.1 What financial well-being is

What emerged in the course of our research is that financial well-being describes a continuum—ranging from severe financial stress to being highly satisfied with one's financial situation—not strictly aligned with income level. For example, some people seem to have, and feel they have, a high level of financial well-being, even though they may be far from affluent. On the other hand, some people with much higher incomes do not appear to have or feel they have a high level of financial well-being at all. Moreover, through learning and effort, and given reasonable opportunity and supports, it appears that people can move along the continuum to greater financial well-being.

> In summary, financial well-being can be defined as a state of being wherein a person can fully meet current and ongoing financial obligations, can feel secure in their financial future, and is able to make choices that allow enjoyment of life.

The definition of financial well-being that we propose is based on the consumer perspective and flows from the open-ended interviews our research team conducted with a broadly diverse set of consumers across the United States, reinforced by interviews with financial practitioners. The specific individual goals and vision of a satisfying life differed greatly among respondents, yet there were two common themes that arose consistently: security and freedom of choice, in the present and in the future.

More specifically, analysis of the interview transcripts and discussion with the panel of experts suggests that the concept of financial well-being has four central elements:

- Having control over day-to-day, month-to-month finances;

- Having the capacity to absorb a financial shock;

- Being on track to meet your financial goals; and

- Having the financial freedom to make the choices that allow you to enjoy life.

These elements of financial well-being have strong time-frame dimensions: the first and fourth pertain mainly to one's present situation, and the second and third elements pertain to securing the future, as discussed below.

FIGURE 1:   THE FOUR ELEMENTS OF FINANCIAL WELL-BEING

	Present	Future
Security	Control over your day-to-day, month-to-month finances	Capacity to absorb a financial shock
Freedom of choice	Financial freedom to make choices to enjoy life	On track to meet your financial goals

3.1.1   Having control over day-to-day, month-to-month finances

Individuals who have a relatively high level of financial well-being feel in control of their day-to-day financial lives. These individuals manage their finances; their finances do not manage them. Such individuals are able to cover expenses and pay bills on time, and do not worry about having enough money to get by. This is the aspect of financial well-being that was mentioned most frequently during the qualitative interviews.

3.1.2   Having the capacity to absorb a financial shock

Individuals who have a relatively high level of financial well-being also have the capacity to absorb a financial shock. Because of a combination of factors such as having a support system of family and friends, owning personal savings, and holding insurance of various types, their lives would not be up-ended if their car or home needed an emergency repair or if they were laid off temporarily from their job. They are able to cope with the financial challenges of unforeseen life events.

3.1.3 Being on track to meet your financial goals

Individuals experiencing financial well-being also say they are on track to meet their financial goals. They have a formal or informal financial plan, and they are actively working toward goals such as saving to buy a car or home, paying off student loans, or saving for retirement.

3.1.4 Having the financial freedom to make choices that allow you to enjoy life

Finally, individuals experiencing financial well-being perceive that they are able to make choices that allow them to enjoy life. They can splurge once in a while. They can afford "wants," such as being able to go out to dinner or take a vacation, in addition to meeting their "needs," and they are able to make choices such as to be generous toward their friends, family and community.

> Traditional measures such as income or net worth, while important, do not fully capture this aspect of the concept of financial well-being.

This fourth element came through strongly in the interviews, and was notable in the variety of ways it was expressed. For example, financial freedom might mean being able to be generous with family, friends and community; or having the ability to go back to school or leave one job to look for a better one; or to go out to dinner or on vacation; or to work less to spend time with family. Because individuals value such different things, traditional measures such as income or net worth, while important, do not fully capture this aspect of the concept of financial well-being. It is these deeply personal preferences and aspirations that give meaning and purpose to the often challenging day-to-day financial decisions and tradeoffs we all must make to achieve it.

3.2 Differences between working-age and older consumer perspectives on financial well-being

Overall, thoughts expressed by working-age and older consumers about the meaning of financial well-being were remarkably similar. As the table below illustrates, eight of the 10 themes most frequently mentioned by each group appeared for both groups, though the intended meanings may have differed somewhat.

TABLE 1: RANKED THEMES ASSOCIATED WITH FINANCIAL WELL-BEING

Rank	Working-age Consumers	Rank	Older Consumers
1	Able to afford "wants"	1	Spouse/partner (knowledge + resource)
2	Family (knowledge + resource)	2	Family (knowledge + resource)
3	Good employment	2	Lack of financial stress/worry
4	Savings	4	Able to pay bills
5	Able to pay bills	4	Having a financial plan
6	Lack of financial stress/worry	6	Able to afford "wants"
7	Spouse/partner (knowledge + resource)	7	Good employment
8	Home ownership (or lack thereof)	8	Afford or have access to healthcare/health insurance
9	Afford or have access to healthcare/health insurance	9	Provide for family
10	Lifestyle	10	Savings

Source: Consumer interviews

For example, older consumers, when they mentioned being on track to meet financial goals, were most often focused on end-of-life expenses or the related issue of whether their savings would last them to the end of their lives. Working-age consumers, on the other hand, were most often focused on preparing for retirement or paying off debt. The two themes that ranked highly only among the working-age cohort but not the older cohort were "home ownership (or lack thereof)" and "lifestyle." Conversely, the older cohort mentioned the themes of "having a financial plan" and "provide for family" more frequently than the working-age cohort did.

Differences in focus between working-age and older consumers were revealed in how often they mentioned the various themes. Access to healthcare and health insurance was brought up more often by the older group, as was the importance of having a financial plan. When family was mentioned in older respondents' interviews, it was generally in the context of avoiding the need for support from the family for the older consumer. Older consumers brought up quality employment somewhat less frequently than working-age consumers did, but it was still one of their most common themes. For example, older consumers often mentioned paid employment in the context of providing a financial cushion (being able to go back to work if their investments performed poorly), or alternatively as a strategy for providing resources to be able to afford vacations and other "wants."

4. What influences individual financial well-being

While the definition of financial well-being that emerged from this research derives solely from qualitative interviews with consumers and financial practitioners, our hypotheses about what likely influences financial well-being come from synthesizing all three methodologies pursued in this project: the review of existing literature, the qualitative interviews, and discussion with academic and practitioner experts.

This section begins with a discussion of the behaviors that, given an individual's opportunities, seem to support financial well-being. To be sure, structural opportunities like macro-economic context, family wealth and connections, access to education, and geographic location play a major role in financial well-being. Such factors create a set of options available to an individual. Our view is that individual behavior interacts with opportunity to produce a resulting level of financial well-being. While opportunity plays a huge role in well-being, our research focuses on the individual factors that support well-being, given a certain level of opportunity. Therefore, our focus is on how do we—the CFPB and others working in financial education and financial capability—help people make the best of their situation? The sections that follow explore different avenues for approaching that question.

We go on to describe the types of knowledge and skills that likely support the identified behaviors, recognizing the existence and influence of mediating factors like decision context[26] and personal traits. We then discuss those personal traits, which include personal attitudes,

---

[26] We are referring here to the widely established Social Psychology principle that human behavior is a function of both the person and the situation in which the action is taken (or not taken). See, e.g. Ross, Lee and Richard E. Nisbett. *The person and the situation: Perspectives of social psychology*. New York, NY: McGraw-Hill Book Company. (1991)

non-cognitive skills, and personality traits, that also appear to support the identified behaviors. Finally we describe what we learned about how social and economic context provides or limits opportunities for achieving financial well-being, and how life stage relates to financial well-being.

4.1 Financial behaviors

The qualitative interview process asked consumers to identify decisions made or not made, and actions taken or not taken, that they felt had influenced their financial well-being. We similarly asked practitioners to describe what their more successful clients tended to do and the kinds of decisions they tended to make, and in many cases practitioners offered their own personal experiences as well.

Through the course of the qualitative research we heard people describe a multitude of strategies that they as consumers have developed and adopted for navigating their financial lives. People flexibly deploy various strategies depending on the problems they encounter or the goals they are trying to achieve. In some cases actions we had thought of as singular, such as "saving," turn out to encompass a wide range of behaviors in consumers' minds. Consumers and practitioners described similar behaviors; the most salient difference was that even though consumers discussed budgeting fairly frequently, financial practitioners even more consistently mentioned and discussed both budgeting and tracking where your money has gone as behaviors or strategies likely to support financial well-being.

Overall, all categories of interviewees—financial practitioners, older consumers, and working-age consumers—tended to organize their responses around similar topics. Those that arose most often included saving, being frugal or cheap, budgeting, buying "needs" and not "wants," managing debt, making sound financial decisions with respect to home ownership, having a financial plan, and investing.

The topics tended to fall into thematic groups—*managing money, research and knowledge-seeking, planning and goal-setting,* and *following through*—used to organize the discussion of their responses below, while acknowledging inevitable overlap in the mapping of responses onto themes. These four themes—the first three of which will look particularly familiar to financial capability researchers and practitioners—form the basis for our hypotheses about the key behaviors that likely support financial well-being. Specifically, it appears that individuals who engage in the following behaviors are more likely to have higher levels of financial well-being.

4.1.1 Behaviors related to effective, routine money management

I think you've got to think restraints, spending restraints. You know, I think that above all. You got to know how much money you have, what's coming in, what's going out, and restrain yourself to what you've got. Make sure you can really manage your debt well. I think that's probably the biggest thing. **- Older consumer, Los Angeles**

While the ability to make conscious financial decisions is likely a key factor in achieving higher levels of financial well-being, most often people rely on unconscious decision-making strategies to navigate their day-to-day financial lives. Effective routine money management encompasses two high level concepts: managing the money that goes out, i.e., "*living within your means*"; and managing the money that comes in, i.e., making sure you have enough income to cover your needs.

Concepts related to living within means

- *Being frugal or cheap.* Interviewees described frugality as a learned skill, usually acquired during one's upbringing or through personal experience. For many, being frugal describes a lifestyle that organizes other behaviors around a central focus of being disciplined and consciously choosing to spend less money, especially early in life to save for retirement. Some reported relying on budgets and other tools to enforce frugality. Many discussed, often in the context of budgeting, the personal importance of differentiating between "needs" and "wants" as a simple binary approach to prioritizing spending, although particulars varied markedly with individuals' social and environmental contexts.

- *Maintaining an intentional lifestyle.* Consumers and practitioners both said that being content with what you have, or dismissing the allure of a free-spending lifestyle, is one way to achieve financial well-being. The focus here is on contentment rather than on sacrifice as with frugality. Some interviewees suggested that a free-spending lifestyle poses a detriment to one's financial well-being because it represents not thinking about the future.

- *Using credit cards prudently if at all.* Many persons interviewed expressed strong opinions about credit cards. Most interviewees believed carrying credit card debt affects financial well-being negatively. In fact when discussing the importance of managing resources effectively on a routine basis, many brought up credit card debt as a specific symptom of failure. Others described carrying credit card debt as a behavior revealing an inability to plan ahead.

- *Avoiding and managing debt.* More generally, many consumers thought of non-mortgage debt as a major threat to their financial well-being. Some described how being in debt made them feel that their finances were out of control. Both consumers and practitioners said that many people are unsure of the best way to effectively manage their debt, but as with other financial behaviors, consumers report gathering information from their social networks and from their own personal experience to develop strategies to fit their own debt situations.

Concepts related to maintaining income

- *Doing whatever it takes to find work.* One of the most commonly mentioned drivers of financial well-being was having stable employment. Many interviewees said that in the event of a job loss it is important to do whatever you have to do to provide for yourself and for your family. For some, this meant taking jobs that they would not normally expect to take, in order to secure a paycheck. Some spoke of doing what it takes to find work as being entrepreneurial and taking risks. Often consumers talked about doing what it takes to find work in the same way they talked about being hardworking or being driven. Consumers often spoke of such focus on bringing in income as a skill they acquired by watching their parents struggle and survive hard times.

- *Using credit for liquidity to avoid loss of earnings.* Some consumers and practitioners felt that credit cards can form part of one's safety net—that having access to credit means one has the financial resources to allow them to continue working in the face of unexpected costs. For example, inability to afford a car repair can compound into loss of employment. Having credit card credit available in such a case can help maintain income.

4.1.2 Behaviors related to researching decisions and seeking knowledge

Yeah, you have to do your research. You have to be willing to read about it. It's not through osmosis. I still like to read an actual newspaper every day, I always read the business section. **- Working-age consumer, Los Angeles**

Okay, cautious means you don't just jump into something, you do your research. Prepared, you've done the research; you've done the planning and have thought about the pros and cons of a particular financial move. So now I'm ready to make that move, to make a decision, either pro or con. **- Working-age consumer, Atlanta**

Consumers reported relying first and foremost on those close to them for financial information. When people face financial questions, they most frequently seek information from family and friends, then cast a wider net. They also learn passively from those close to them; interviewees reported observing and learning from both positive and negative examples of behaviors from those around them. Many reported having an identified financial go-to person among the people they know.

- *Relying on family and spouse for knowledge.* Spouses or partners in particular were described as a valuable source of financial knowledge because they can offer a different perspective and serve as a trusted sounding board. For many working-age consumers, parents were seen as particularly useful because they are trusted and understand their children's specific context. Older consumers similarly felt that their children provide valuable financial guidance. Such advice from (and to) one's family members or spouse is often exchanged by way of informal conversations. Some consumers solicit advice by asking specifically what seems like the best option or how they should go about engaging in a particular financial behavior. Others use their family members simply as sounding boards in order to feel more confident they are doing the right sorts of things and making the best choices.

- *Watching others or seeking advice from others.* People commonly described the importance of more broadly using those around them as resources—including in a negative sense: many described gaining knowledge from observing the mistakes of people they know. For example, many people talked about soliciting advice from extended family and from friends in their social networks. For others just having such acquaintances to use as a sounding board was important. Consumers commonly mentioned seeking out information when it comes time to make plans for investing, saving strategies, buying a car, or buying a home; but many also brought up how challenging they felt it was to find someone they could trust to give them financial advice.

- *Doing formal financial research.* Consumers and practitioners agreed that doing formal financial research, in the sense of studying a topic or looking it up, is important. Many consumers, however, said they felt intimidated by the sheer volume of financial information available and often "did not know where to start." With this in mind, many defined doing formal research as the dual act of seeking out information and then evaluating its fit for one's particular situation. How and where people reported doing formal financial research varied. Some read books by popular financial professionals. Others read the business section of the newspaper regularly. Some said that when they need information they can go to the library. Many interviewees said that almost anything you need to know is available on the internet. Finally, some consumers reach out to a financial professional either as a source of knowledge or to use as a sounding board.

- *Getting a good education as a route to financial literacy.* In addition to its other benefits, interviewees felt that education, even when not explicitly financial in content, provides knowledge—including knowledge about how to do research—that allows one to make better-informed financial decisions. Research supports this notion: indicators of general knowledge such as years of education have proven to be highly correlated with positive consumer financial behavior and outcomes, such as having a higher credit score and reduced likelihood of experiencing bankruptcy or foreclosure.[27]

4.1.3 Behaviors related to financial goal-setting and planning

Well, the reason I said retirement and not short-term because I have watched too many people that have retired that I have talked to and they've said, "Look, we've retired now

---

[27] Cole, Shawn Allen and Paulson, Anna L. and Shastry, Gauri Kartini, "Smart Money: The Effect of Education on Financial Behavior" (April 11, 2012). Harvard Business School Finance Working Paper No. 09-071.

and we don't have any money to fall back on." They didn't think ahead like me.
- Working-age consumer, Washington, D.C.

Financial security in a short statement is – it means that you are not going to panic if something happens. Most people starting don't have that luxury so you've got to plan for it. Have to plan for it. **- Older consumer, Wyoming**

Financial practitioners and consumers alike felt one has to be future oriented in order to achieve financial well-being. Future orientation manifests itself in behaviors such as planning, financial goal setting, and budgeting. Research has found that future oriented, planning behaviors are associated with an array of positive financial outcomes.[28]

- *Budgeting.* Many interviewees reported using some form of budget, although the ways people go about creating and adhering to budgets vary widely. Some consumers develop very short-term, week-to-week budgets, while others focus on a longer time horizon. Having a budget made interviewees feel more secure because it gives them something against which to track where their money goes even when they don't adhere to it—that is, even when they do not actually succeed at the money-management aspect of having a budget.

- *Having financial goals.* The importance of having a financial goal arose as a topic in a majority of the qualitative interviews. For many, a financial goal gave meaning to particular financial behaviors such as saving or creating a budget. However, consumers and practitioners alike stated—and the health behavior change literature[29] reinforces—that financial goals only affect behavior if they feel realistic and attainable; financial practitioners commonly said that the hardest task for most people is to set realistic financial goals. Some of the consumers and practitioners also suggested that the kinds of financial strategies that an individual adopts are guided by the kinds of financial goals that they set for themselves. Many working-age consumers set long-term goals, like having a secure retirement or paying off their mortgage. Others set shorter-term goals,

---

[28] Lynch, John G. Jr., Richard G. Netemeyer, Stephen A. Spiller, and Alessandra Zammit. "A generalizable scale of propensity to plan: The long and the short of planning for time and for money." *Journal of Consumer Research.* 37(1) (2010): 108–128.
[29] See the National Institutes of Health "Guide to Behavior Change," available at https://www.nhlbi.nih.gov/health/educational/lose_wt/behavior.htm (accessed October 31, 2014.)

like paying off credit card debt. Some consumers spoke of goals such as travel or a new car that guided their financial behavior. As people's situations change over time, so do their goals. For example some people said their financial goals changed after they had children. Older Americans' financial plans tended to involve ensuring they didn't spend down their savings before they passed on, and making sure they had the financial resources or insurance to afford end-of-life care.

- *Having a financial plan.* Many people similarly talked about the importance of having a financial plan to manage one's spending. In this sense a financial plan is seen as encompassing all of the strategies and behaviors consumers employ to achieve their goals. Interviewees differentiated between financial plans and budgets; they thought of financial plans as longer-term and as more general than household budgets, which are seen more as an immediate tool to keep spending habits in line with plans. Both consumers and practitioners agreed that having a financial plan requires having a financial goal.

- *Getting a good education as a financial plan.* Interviewees suggested that one of the best things one can do for oneself to promote financial well-being is to get a good education. Many noted that income and education are positively correlated, and talked about education opening doors to higher paying, more stable employment. Younger working consumers in particular said that getting an education was very important—but that taking out the necessary student loans has negatively affected their financial well-being.

4.1.4 Behaviors related to following through on decisions and intentions

Create a plan. Well, first—be realistic. Being realistic in where you are in your life at that given time. And then creating a plan short term to mid-term and long term to get to the point where you want to be. And then, you know, take steps a little bit at a time to get there. **- Financial Practitioner, Los Angeles**

Interviewees clearly recognized the gulf between deciding and executing, between intending to adopt a strategy or alter a behavior and successfully carrying through with the intention. The idea they expressed is that often it is after we gather reliable information to study, or after we fully comprehend the ramifications of a financial topic, or after we have reached a logical, well-intentioned and informed decision, or after we have decided on a rational plan—or even after we have embarked on our plan—that we fail.

- *Saving.* Consumers and practitioners alike spoke about the importance of saving as a means of securing one's future and protecting against unforeseen expenses. For many, saving is a conscious decision and a daily activity—but one that in practice encompasses several execution skills and rigorously followed habits chosen according to individuals' circumstances and time horizons. "Saving" for some interviewees meant literally depositing money in a bank account; for others it meant spending less or comparison shopping, investing generally or, for many working-age consumers, investing in a retirement account. Consumers and practitioners both brought up budgeting as an important saving strategy, but it requires following through on intentions to turn budgets into money saved.

- *Investing.* Many interviewees felt that investing is critical to both long- and short-term wealth creation, and is thus a key ingredient in securing one's financial future. People with and without investments both expressed this view. As with savings, interviewees described a range of intentional behaviors, carried through diligently, as "investments," including participation in the stock market, purchasing real estate, starting a business, and more. One practitioner suggested that *all* purchases should be viewed as investments, as a way of encouraging people to think more strategically about how they spend their money.

- *Getting a good education as a task to complete.* As noted, interviewees felt that one of the best things one can do for oneself financially is to make sure to get a good education, and in part this implies following through with completing an educational goal as an investment in your future earning potential. Interviewees also talked about how being future oriented when young enables one to make better decisions with respect to engaging in or completing one's education.

4.2 Financial knowledge

For this research project, we have focused on trying to understand what kind of knowledge is most likely to influence financial behavior, and how it does so. We reviewed existing research on the connection between knowledge and behavior from a number of different fields. We also asked our interview respondents to share with us the most valuable financial lessons they had learned over the years, where they learned those lessons, and what information had proven most helpful in their financial decision making. We similarly asked financial practitioners to identify the knowledge they considered most important for their clients to have.

> Factual knowledge in and of itself is not sufficient to drive behavior or behavior change.

Our first key finding in this area is that factual knowledge in and of itself is not sufficient to drive behavior or behavior change.[30] Our review of existing literature suggests that the link between knowledge and behavior is always mediated by individual characteristics like attitudes and non-cognitive skills, and by the context in which a decision is made or action is taken.[31] Even when one possesses knowledge of a topic, whether that knowledge is processed in such a way as to inform behavior depends on a number of intermediary factors: personal efficacy; subjective norms (one's perception of what is appropriate or expected); one's attitude toward the contemplated behavior; and one's intention.

---

[30] Ajzen, I., N. Joyce, S. Sheikh, and N. Gilbert-Cote. "Knowledge and the prediction of behavior: the role of information accuracy in the theory of planned behavior." Basic and Applied Social Psychology 33 (2011): 101-117.

Kiviat, Barbara, and Jonathan Morduch. "From financial literacy to financial action." Financial Access Initiative: Robert F. Wagner Graduate School of Public Service, New York University, and McGraw-Hill Research Foundation. http://www.mhfigi.com/wp-content/uploads/2013/08/Financial_Literacy_WP.pdf (2012) (accessed October 10th, 2014).

Robb, Cliff A., and Ann S. Woodyard. "Financial knowledge and best practice behavior." Journal of Financial Counseling and Planning. 22(1) (2011): 60–70.

Mandell, Lewis, and Linda Schmid Klein. "The Impact of Financial Literacy Education on Subsequent Financial Behavior." Journal of Financial Counseling and Planning. 20(1) (2009): 15–24.

Serido, Joyce, Soyeon Shim, and Chuanyi Tang. "A developmental model of financial capability: A framework for promoting a successful transition to adulthood." International Journal of Behavioral Development 37(4) (2013): 287–297.

[31] Thaler, Richard H., and Cass R. Sunstein. Nudge: Improving Decisions About Health, Wealth, and Happiness. New Haven: Yale University Press. (2008).

Duflo, Esther, and Emmanuel Saez. "Participation and investment decisions in a retirement plan: The influence of colleagues' choices." Journal of Public Economics. 85(1) (2002): 121–148.

Duflo, Esther, and Emmanuel Saez. "The role of information and social interactions in retirement plan decisions: Evidence from a randomized experiment." Quarterly Journal of Economics 118(3) (2003): 815–842.

Bettman, James R., and C. Whan Park. "Effects of prior knowledge and experience and phase of the choice process on consumer decision processes: A protocol analysis." Journal of Consumer Research. 7(3) (1980): 234–248.

Costanzo, Mark, Dane Archer, Elliot Aronson, and Thomas Pettigrew. "Energy conservation behavior: The difficult path from information to action." American Psychologist. 41(5) (1986): 521–528.

Holden, Karen. "The emotions and cognitions behind financial decisions: The implications of theory for practice." Center for Financial Security. http://www.cfs.wisc.edu/papers/Holden2010_EmotionsPaper.pdf (2010) (accessed October 10th, 2014).

In addition, while this report focuses on the behaviors and attributes of individuals, the importance of decision context—the domain of social psychology and behavioral economics—must be acknowledged. Context structures opportunity and influences individual choices. For example, employers who offer automatic payroll deduction into a retirement account provide their employees with a simple, streamlined way to save; however, individuals who do not have this infrastructure provided for them must take additional steps to save, which reduces the likelihood that they will do so.[32]

In the course of the qualitative research, both consumers and practitioners were far more likely to mention the importance of knowing *how* to do things than knowledge of particular facts. Fundamentally, the concept of skill means knowing how to do things, not just knowing what they are. The primary hypothesis in the financial knowledge domain suggested by our research is that the type of knowledge most likely to support or predict financial behaviors supportive of financial well-being—holding mediating factors constant—is a set of skills we call "financial ability."

4.2.1 Financial ability

Our research suggests that the concept of financial ability, as defined below, captures in a general sense the "skill" component that is widely understood to be a key element of financial literacy and capability. The finding is not that domain-specific knowledge is not needed by consumers in specific situations and for particular tasks: clearly it is. The point is rather that domain-specific knowledge per se is not a comprehensive indicator of financial skill for all people in all situations and life stages.

Financial ability is conceptualized as the set of skills that supports the behaviors identified in the prior section on financial behaviors and strategies, and encompasses:

- Knowing when to seek out and where to find reliable information to make a financial decision;

- Knowing how to process financial information to make sound financial decisions; and,

---

[32] Madrian, Brigitte C., and Dennis F. Shea. "The power of suggestion: Inertia in 401(k) participation and savings behavior. *The Quarterly Journal of Economics*. 116(4) (2001): 1149–1187.

- Knowing how to execute financial decisions, including monitoring and adapting as necessary to stay on track.

People with strong financial ability know where to start looking for the information they need to make a financial decision—whether that information is advice from an experienced friend, multiple quotes for a mortgage, or professional investment advice. Once they obtain financial information, persons with financial ability know how to process it—for example, they know how to run the numbers to figure out which auto loan would work best for their budget. And finally, people with financial ability know how to get themselves to execute and stick to their financial plans over the long term and adjust those plans as necessary.

Financial literacy has an action component—the ability or skills to put financial knowledge to use.

A growing consensus in the broader financial literature[33] also appears to point toward this wider notion of financial ability: the idea that in addition to a knowledge or information component, financial literacy has an action component—that is, the ability or skills to put financial knowledge to use. The dual elements of knowledge and action in CFPB's own mandate to "improve the financial literacy of consumers" and "educate and empower consumers to make better informed financial decisions" reflects this growing understanding.

Ultimately, neither information, knowledge, deciding, planning, nor even starting on a course of action is alone sufficient to succeed in a task. Beyond good beginnings we face the immense human challenge of following through with the next step and the next, despite challenges and distractions. What our interviewees expressed is the notion that overcoming that challenge is a skill—a skill like any other for which a person may have an inborn aptitude, but which for most people requires learning and mastering.

This ability—to get oneself to do whatever it takes to make desired choices repeatedly—is critical to success in a wide range of finance-related behaviors that require discipline: behaving frugally, actively saving, making the time to research and plan, adhering to a budget, resisting impulsive

---

[33] Examples include:
Atkinson, Adele, Stephen McKay, Sharon Collard, and Elaine Kempson. "Levels of financial capability in the UK." Public Money and Management. 27(1) (2007): 29–36.
OECD Programme for International Student Assessment. PISA 2012 Assessment and Analytical Framework: Mathematics, Reading, Science, Problem Solving and Financial Literacy. http://dx.doi.org/10.1787/9789264190511-en(2013) (accessed October 10th, 2014).

purchases or lifestyle-related temptations or simple "wants." Accomplishing a goal or other desired behavior is rarely a matter of just doing it, but also of knowing how to get oneself to do it. In the course of the qualitative research, consumers and practitioners shared a number of techniques that have worked for them in their financial lives and the importance to them and to their financial well-being of having acquired that skill.

What influences financial ability?

How do people develop the financial skills and expertise they do have? Some of our interviewees, both consumers and practitioners, said that schools, from primary through trade schools and college, should emphasize financial education and literacy to a greater extent, and there is research to support this view.[34] Many of them, based on either their own experience or the observations of others, clearly felt that young adults often lack the financial ability they need to succeed. At the same

> Upbringing, social context, and personal networks promote familiarity with and confidence in key skills and behaviors.

time, when reflecting on their own experiences, the interviewees suggested that other modes of learning and types of knowledge had influenced their level of financial ability. Instead of formal financial knowledge, they placed major emphasis on the roles of upbringing, social context, or personal networks in providing experiential learning that promotes familiarity with and confidence in key skills and behaviors.

Upbringing was one of the themes brought up most often in the qualitative interviews, and many saw upbringing as their most important source of learning practical financial ability (though interestingly, no older consumers mentioned "upbringing" in their list of most

---

[34] Brown, Meta and van der Klaauw, Wilbert and Wen, Jaya and Zafar, Basit. "Financial Education and the Debt Behavior of the Young." (September 2013). FRB of New York Staff Report No. 634.

Brown, Alexandra J., Michael Collins, Maximilian Schmeiser, and Carly Urban. "State Mandated Financial Education and the Credit Behavior of Young Adults." Finance and Economics Discussion Series, Federal Reserve Board, Washington, D.C. 2014-68.

Serido, Joyce, Soyeon Shim, and Chuanyi Tang. "A developmental model of financial capability: A framework for promoting a successful transition to adulthood." *International Journal of Behavioral Development*. 37(4) (2013): 287–297.

Shim, Soyeon, Jing J. Xiao, Bonnie L. Barber, and Angela C. Lyons. "Pathways to life success: A conceptual model of financial well-being for young adults." *Journal of Applied Developmental Psychology*. 30(6) (2009): 708–723.

important factors affecting financial well-being). Watching one's parents navigate their financial lives deeply informs how one navigates one's own financial life—one absorbs not only financial facts, but also behaviors, skills, and contextual cultural norms about money. Interviewees did not always follow in their parents' financial footsteps: many noted that upbringing can teach and reinforce bad behaviors just as easily as good behaviors; and for some, watching their parents or others struggle motivated them to lead their own financial lives differently.

Many consumers reported that they gained much of their financial ability through personal experiences or the experiences of persons in their personal networks or broader social contexts, in particular from mistakes they or others had made. This was especially true of early experience with credit cards. Consumers noted that those bad decisions, as long as they were not too extreme, were critical to improving their financial well-being because they learned from them.

Many of the financial behaviors that consumers described as beneficial for financial well-being are strategies they synthesize from financial information gathered from different sources and from personal experience. "Correct" or "beneficial" financial behaviors are often communicated in the form of rules of thumb, such as "pay yourself first." Some consumers talked about learning rules of thumb from their parents as part of their upbringing; others develop their own or pick them up from peers or others. Teaching rules of thumb has been shown to influence financial behavior.[35] This fits with what we know from other research: decision-makers are apt to use the information available or accessible at the moment of decision, like a remembered rule of thumb, rather than pausing to engage in research.[36]

Finally, in the very broadest sense, one's level of general knowledge is positively correlated with positive financial behaviors.[37] This finding suggests that perhaps one's general scope of knowledge and skill, everything acquired from family and others, from personal experience, and from formal education quite apart from the specialized financial expertise one gains, may enhance one's financial ability.

---

[35] Drexler, Alejandro, Greg Fischer, and Antoinette Schoar. "Keeping it simple: Financial literacy and rules of thumb." *American Economic Journal: Applied Economics*. 6(2) (2014): 1–31.

[36] Tversky, Amos, and Daniel Kahneman. "Judgment under uncertainty: Heuristics and biases." *Science*. 185(4157) (1974): 1124–1131.

[37] Cole, Shawn Allen and Paulson, Anna L. and Shastry, Gauri Kartini, "Smart Money: The Effect of Education on Financial Behavior" (April 11, 2012). Harvard Business School Finance Working Paper No. 09-071.

4.3 Personal traits

Personal attitudes, non-cognitive skills, and personality traits, which we refer to collectively as personal traits, all influence behavior directly and play a role in mediating the connection between knowledge and behavior. These might include, for example, whether a person is *driven*, is a *planner,* is *materialistic*, or possesses that quality often termed "*grit*"—a propensity to persevere in the face of challenges. Although humans appear to be born with many such personality-related characteristics already defined—or defined so early in life that it is difficult to know whether they were in-born or not—certain of these attributes remain quite malleable for a time,[38] or in some cases appear to be more malleable during certain windows of time in childhood or youth.[39] Regardless of their malleability, it is important to state and test hypotheses about the role of these characteristics in order make sure that tests of the role of other factors, such as knowledge and skills, control for the relevant personal traits.

Several such personal traits particularly relevant to financial well-being emerged in our qualitative research or have been identified in other research, particularly in the fields of cognitive psychology and cognitive neuroscience. These include attitudes and non-cognitive skills that mediate the transmission of factual knowledge into behavior, or in some cases drive behavior on their own. Research suggests they could potentially be influenced—to varying degrees and at different times of life—by well-designed programs, opportunities and supports. We discuss them below, divided into four groups.

---

[38] Moffitt, Terrie E., Louise Arseneault, Daniel Belsky, Nigel Dickson, Robert J. Hancox, HonaLee Harrington, Renate Houts, Richie Poulton, Brent W. Roberts, Stephen Ross, Malcolm R. Sears, W. Murray Thomson, and Avshalom Caspi. "A gradient of childhood self-control predicts health, wealth, and public safety." *Proceedings of the National Academy of Sciences.* 108(7) (2011): 2693–2698.
Pathak, Payal, Jamie Holmes, and Jamie Zimmerman. "Accelerating financial capability among youth: Nudging new thinking." New America Foundation.
http://www.newamerica.net/sites/newamerica.net/files/policydocs/AcceleratingFinancialCapabilityamongYouth.pdf (2011) (accessed October 10th, 2014).
[39] Moffitt, Terrie E., Louise Arseneault, Daniel Belsky, Nigel Dickson, Robert J. Hancox, HonaLee Harrington, Renate Houts, Richie Poulton, Brent W. Roberts, Stephen Ross, Malcolm R. Sears, W. Murray Thomson, and Avshalom Caspi. "A gradient of childhood self-control predicts health, wealth, and public safety." *Proceedings of the National Academy of Sciences.* 108(7) (2011): 2693–2698.

4.3.1 Internal frame of reference

How do you judge your own success? Do you compare yourself to others, or, in the words of some of our interviewees, do you measure yourself by your own yardstick? The latter reflects having an internal frame of reference, a well-researched topic in the psychology literature that also emerged from our qualitative research interviews, signifying strong awareness of the concept in the public mind. Interviewees appeared to see this characteristic or attitude as learned, sometimes as children from one's family or social context, sometimes, perhaps with more difficulty, as adults.

Many interviewees equated low self-esteem—that is, judging oneself harshly in comparison with others—with emotion-driven spending; they saw being insecure or not feeling good about oneself as leading to impulsive spending or spending to make yourself feel better in the moment. Respondents often referenced frame of reference in the context of talking about frugality, indicating that making do with less requires ignoring social pressure, and that some people are better able to do this than others, and that such frugality is a skill that one often learns to feel proud of as a personal attribute during one's upbringing or from one's spouse or partner.

Others referenced social pressure directly. A number of interviewees described materialism as a form of giving in to external social pressures. Many framed social pressure as "needing to keep up with the Joneses" and identified it as one reason people overspend. Some respondents described the ability to not give in to outside perceptions as critical to financial well-being.

4.3.2 Perseverance

Drive, grit, perseverance, and being a hard worker, which we refer to together as perseverance, are words offered by respondents in our qualitative research that all refer to complex attributes that may, in combination with other aspects of personality and habit, define highly motivated people. Cognitive researchers share our respondents' interest, although vocabularies may differ: for example, the scientific concept of "willingness to persevere" relates to the concept of "grit" described by respondents. Such attributes are a function of both genes and experience.[40]

---

[40] Duckworth, Angela. "Can Perseverance Be Taught?" Big Questions Online (August 5, 2013). *Available at:* https://www.bigquestionsonline.com/content/can-perseverance-be-taught.

Many of those interviewed felt that hard-working or conscientious individuals are more likely to achieve financial well-being. Some felt that being hard-working leads to more opportunities in the workplace; others used the concept in more personal terms to signify actions like having a spending plan or using a budget consistently over time. Interviewees also used the word "driven" to describe individuals who are highly motivated to achieve a goal such as saving or budgeting. Driven individuals were also perceived as more likely to overcome adversity.

More generally, some interviewees suggested that individuals who are more inherently responsible will have better abilities to, for example, distinguish between needs and wants, pay their bills on time, not fall into debt, or avoid risky behaviors such as over-reliance on credit cards.

4.3.3   Executive functioning

Particularly relevant to behaviors supportive of financial well-being are personal attributes that relate to *executive function*, a multifaceted suite of mental operations involved in self-control, planning, and focus that are seated, in neurological terms, primarily in the late-maturing pre-frontal cortex of the human brain.[41] Several such attributes are strongly involved in the kinds of personal characteristics and attitudes that relate to financial well-being. The fact that they are late-maturing opens the possibility of designing effective approaches to help children's and young adults' brains mature optimally to establish strong executive function-related attributes.

> Being a planner and having good self-control have been shown to relate directly to executive function.

Several characteristics that were mentioned by respondents, such as being a planner or having good self-control, have been shown in current research to relate directly to executive function. Interviewees often expressed the idea that having a plan for coping with unforeseen events or shocks is critical to achieving financial well-being, or referenced planning more generally,

---

[41] Moffitt, Terrie E., Louise Arseneault, Daniel Belsky, Nigel Dickson, Robert J. Hancox, HonaLee Harrington, Renate Houts, Richie Poulton, Brent W. Roberts, Stephen Ross, Malcolm R. Sears, W. Murray Thomson, and Avshalom Caspi. "A gradient of childhood self-control predicts health, wealth, and public safety." *Proceedings of the National Academy of Sciences.* 108(7) (2011): 2693–2698.

touching on the cognitive-science concepts of being future-oriented and having a propensity to plan.

Similarly, people reported constantly feeling tempted to spend rather than save; respondents felt that achieving financial well-being requires sufficient self-discipline to make choices that support their financial goals. Having self-control and not being impulsive are both well recognized aspects of executive function, as is managing risk. Figuring out how to balance risk was another common theme in the interviews. Many respondents recognized that financial behaviors such as investing are inherently risky, but nonetheless considered them important to achieving financial well-being.

4.3.4 Financial self-efficacy

Finally, we highlight a key topic drawn from the psychology literature that, although it did not come up directly in the consumer interviews, has been shown in other research to affect financial behavior. Self-efficacy describes a person's confidence in her ability to influence her life outcomes. In the context of financial behavior, this means confidence in one's ability to manage finances without being overwhelmed,[42] including one's perception of one's own ability to achieve financial goals or stick to a spending plan. Efficacious people have an internal locus of control, meaning a belief that they themselves can influence their life outcomes, which underpins their belief in their ability to complete financial tasks and reach financial goals. Conversely, believing one is not in control of the forces that shape one's life—having an external locus of control—is associated with less responsible financial behavior and weakens the positive relationship between financial knowledge and financial behavior,[43] depending to some degree on social contextual factors.

Individuals who have higher levels of financial self-efficacy may be more likely to act on their financial knowledge and, for example, start a business or invest in the stock market.[44] In our

---

[42] Lown, Jean M. "Development and validation of a financial self-efficacy scale" (2011 Outstanding AFCPE® Conference Paper). *Journal of Financial Counseling and Planning.* 22(2) (2012): 54–63.

[43] Perry, Vanessa Gail, and Marlene D. Morris. "Who is in control? The role of self-perception, knowledge, and income in explaining consumer financial behavior." *The Journal of Consumer Affairs.* 39(2) (2006): 299–313.

[44] Chen, Gilad, Stanley M. Gulley, and Dov Eden. "Validation of a new general self-efficacy scale." *Organizational Research Methods.* 4(1) (2001): 62–83.

study, consumers tended to discuss self-esteem in the contexts in which practitioners were more likely to use the term financial self-efficacy.

Taken together, all of these various personal characteristics and traits, when viewed broadly from the dual perspectives of popular understanding as revealed in our qualitative research and emerging scientific findings in the fields of cognitive psychology and cognitive neuroscience, describe a set of hypotheses about how particular traits, attitudes, and non-cognitive skills appear to support or predict financial well-being. This suggests fascinating possibilities for meaningful research into interventions that could powerfully enable individuals to achieve and maintain financial well-being.

4.4 Social and economic environment

Our respondents brought up many examples of social and economic contextual dynamics that they believe are important influences on financial well-being. They often referenced family, friends, community, upbringing, their home life, and many aspects of the world we live in as sources of financial knowledge, examples of positive and negative financial behaviors, and much more. Our interviewees referenced society broadly as shaping us through mass culture, social media, government programs and policies, advertising media[45] that tempt us to indulge ourselves to the detriment of our financial well-being, and in other ways. Our respondents also frequently acknowledged the importance, for themselves or others, of benefits or resources that may help support people's lives in difficult times. Examples included rent-controlled housing, social security, and unemployment insurance.

Some respondents also expressed the belief that chance steps into our lives in many ways. The economy—how our personal life trajectories happen to align with business cycles and other dynamics of the economy—was mentioned as profoundly influencing people's lives. Good employment (especially with benefits) was viewed by many consumers and practitioners as one

> **Good employment was viewed as one of the key drivers of financial well-being.**

---

[45] The CFPB's report 2013 report "Navigating the Market" found that for every dollar put towards financial education in the United States, $25 is spent on financial marketing, which can make it difficult for consumers to find objective information. *Available at:* http://files.consumerfinance.gov/f/201311_cfpb_navigating-the-market-final.pdf.

of the key drivers of financial well-being, yet one that does have an element of luck associated with it.

Life events such as accidents, health and sickness, births and deaths, marriage and divorce, were mentioned as things that can change our financial lives significantly and often without warning, and have also been noted by researchers. [46] Interviewees expressed concern about their ability to cope financially with major life events; older consumers were particularly concerned that end-of-life events could force them to drain their savings and become financially dependent upon family members.

4.5   Life stages

4.5.1   Differences between working-age and older consumer perspectives

A number of thematic differences emerged between the outlooks of working-age and older consumers during the course of the qualitative research interviews. Many of these differences related to life-stage issues, but a few instead reflected the period of history with which their lives coincide, and the life experiences they have had and continue to have as a result.

Older individuals had much more to say about the financial realities of retirement, especially savings and investments, abrupt financial challenges like health crises, and end-of-life expenses (including cognitive decline); and they also frequently discussed, with the benefit of hindsight, the decisions and choices they had made earlier in life that affect their situation now that they are older, such as saving effectively or failing to do so. Many working-age individuals also expressed awareness of issues surrounding retirement savings, but they tended to focus more on immediate mid-life challenges such as losing a job, experiencing a health crisis within their

---

[46] Brobeck, Stephen. "Understanding the emergency savings needs of low- and moderate-income households." Consumer Federation of America. Manuscript available at
http://www.csrees.usda.gov/nea/economics/pdfs/understandingTheEmergencySavingsNeedsOfLow_102908.pdf
(2008) (accessed October 13, 2014).
Chase, Stephanie, Leah Gjertson, and J. Michael Collins. "Coming up with cash in a pinch: Emergency savings and its alternatives." Center for Financial Security. Available at
www.cfs.wisc.edu/briefs/chasegjertsoncollins2011_cashpaper.pdf (2011) (accessed October 13, 2014).

immediate family, or paying for their children's education. Among younger respondents, student loan debt loomed large among their concerns.

Working-age consumers tended to feel more strongly that one's job and one's education level were more critical to financial well-being than older consumers did. Older consumers expressed more awareness of the life-altering effect that a single unexpected life event can have on one's situation. Otherwise, however, working-age Americans and older Americans for the most part identified very similar sets of life forces that enable or hinder financial well-being.

4.5.2   Starting early in life

Both older and working-age consumers stressed the difficulty of changing one's habits or significantly improving one's fundamental financial abilities as an adult. People arrive at adulthood, they implied, with their financial personae already defined. To the extent that this is true, the behaviors, habits, and attitudes developed in youth, positive and negative, appear to strongly affect adult financial well-being. For instance, once one reaches adulthood, there are some changes that one might wish to make, but in many arenas the possibility of actually doing so becomes, according to our respondents, progressively smaller with time.

> Behaviors, habits, and attitudes developed in youth appear to strongly affect adult financial well-being.

This also suggests that the capabilities, knowledge and understanding, personal attributes, and other tools that can positively influence or enable helpful financial behaviors for attaining a high level of financial well-being—these aspects of what one brings from youth into adulthood—are with them to stay. Since many are learned, or at least remain malleable for a time in youth, [47] it provides encouragement for the efforts that the CFPB and others are focusing on youth financial capability. From the viewpoint of the CFPB, this is critical as we turn from this initial phase of looking at adults toward examining, in a next phase of research, the processes that, during childhood and youth, dominate the formation of people's financial-behavior personae.

---

[47] Kautz, Tim, James J. Heckman, Ron Diris, Bas ter Weel, and Lex Borghans. "Fostering and Measuring Skills: Impoving cognitive and non-cognitive skills to promote lifetime success." National Bureau of Economic Research, Working Paper No. 20749 (December 2014).

5. Discussion

The CFPB aims for this research to open a conversation with practitioners, researchers, policymakers and other stakeholders toward collectively establishing a set of best practices in financial literacy and capability that are grounded in evidence-based research. The initial research we report here offers a new way to understand the ultimate goal of financial education: financial well-being. By identifying behaviors, skills and traits that likely lead to improved financial well-being, it suggests potentially effective pathways for strategies and approaches that can develop and sustain financial literacy among consumers.

The research we report here reflects a first step. We do not yet offer quantitative data, or specific guidance on how to implement new strategies or programs. Moving this research forward effectively and thoughtfully will require many thoughtful participants. We want feedback. We need others to innovate, iterate, and help to take this work forward.

With that in mind, we believe the important contributions of this project are:

- A consumer-derived definition of financial well-being;

- Testable hypotheses about the personal characteristics and attitudes that support positive financial behaviors; and

- A concept of "financial ability" to explain how knowledge supports financial behavior.

The foremost implication of our findings is that we need to reframe our understanding of what it means to improve financial literacy. Our research tells us that increasing consumers' knowledge of financial facts is not enough. Rather, in order to reach the end goal of increased financial well-being, we need to help consumers develop the skills,

> **We need to reframe our understanding of what it means to improve financial literacy.**

experience and familiarity, and self-confidence to meaningfully engage in those behaviors that will help increase their financial well-being. With a definition of financial well-being, we now have a clear target to move toward.

5.1 Implications for financial capability practitioners

Financial capability practitioners are uniquely positioned to motivate and empower the people they interact with to engage in behaviors to improve their financial well-being—by connecting those behaviors to their personal goals and aspirations, by evoking their personal vision of a "good life," and by fanning their sense of purpose. Practitioners can empower consumers by helping them develop key skills, offering proven strategies, and sharing the experiences of many others. They can help people connect their goals to financial plans, their plans to day-to-day behaviors, and their behaviors to decisions carried through to completion.

Because knowledge alone does not automatically equate to behavior, the practitioner and client alike must pay attention to the key attitudes and beliefs that will enable the client to engage in the behaviors that will allow them to succeed. A financial advisor needs to think like a personal trainer. For example, does the client possess the skills that define financial ability—that is, the ability to translate financial intentions into financial actions? These include knowing how to:

- Obtain reliable financial information;

- Process financial information to make sound financial decisions; and

- Execute financial decisions, monitoring and adapting as necessary to stay on track.

Similarly, does the client have the attitudes, structural opportunity, and decision context conducive to taking an action? The following diagram shows how multiple factors interact to influence an individual's level of financial well-being.

FIGURE 2:   WHAT INFLUENCES FINANCIAL WELL-BEING

Based on our framework of factors that influence financial well-being, to make it likely that a person will accomplish something, a person needs to:

- Know how to do it (knowledge and skills);

- Feel confident in knowing how to do it effectively (attitude);

- Believe that doing it is valuable (attitude);

- Have the opportunity to do it (opportunity); and

- Encounter a decision context that is conducive to doing it (decision context).

All ways of gaining knowledge are not equally powerful. Experiential learning and just-in-time learning, in the sense of being immediately decision-relevant, are likely to be far more powerful ways for people to gain functional skills than financial learning encountered without any immediate applicability.

Finally, informal influences are tremendously important to most people's financial lives. With or without a financial practitioner to use as a resource, people overwhelmingly get most of both their factual and their normative knowledge about financial topics from their family, their friends, and their community.

Overall, we encourage practitioners to take these ideas and consider how they might be incorporated into your one-on-one interaction strategies or program designs. The field needs practitioners to experiment inventively—and to report back on what you are learning.

5.2 Implications for research

The most salient conclusion for research is the need for more work in this area. The literature review showed that sample sizes in most studies are small, control groups are often lacking, longitudinal studies are rare, and very few, overall, establish causation. Furthermore, the interviews with consumers and practitioners together with our interdisciplinary synthesis of existing literature bring to our attention a new array of concepts, and new ways of thinking and explaining financial knowledge, behaviors and outcomes that require further research.

In particular, we envision work in three areas:

- *Measurability of key concepts.* To judge how and whether changes occur in key skills, attitudes, and behaviors—and in financial well-being itself—in response to interventions or simply over time, we need to be able to quantify those conceptsin a meaningful way. This means, in some cases, measuring what people do, which is standard in consumer finance. But measuring attitudes is a more novel direction in the field of financial education. And we presently have no tools to directly measure key concepts like financial ability and financial well-being. Acquiring them will require completion of an iterative evidence-based development process that we currently have underway.

- *Personal factors as predictors.* From our qualitative research and literature reviews, abetted by the experience and knowledge of our expert panel, we have compiled an extensive list of personal skills, attitudes, habits, behaviors and other individual attributes that are hypothesized to affect financial well-being to some degree. They, and other hypotheses of interest to others in the field about different potential drivers of financial well-being, need to be tested, with the goal of determining which are most predictive of well-being, for whom, and under what circumstances.

- *Success of interventions.* As a field, we need to develop innovative programs and interventions and specifically test them (and our implementation strategies) in terms of their efficacy—their efficacy in supporting the development of the key factors we have identified that may lead to and underlie financial well-being, and their efficacy in improving financial well-being itself.

Using the findings of the research reported here, the CFPB is committed to furthering its consumer financial literacy mission through fostering approaches grounded in an understanding of financial well-being as a key measure of effective financial education. This work presents new pathways and opportunities to move consumer financial capability practices forward in ways that can broadly benefit American consumers, and, through their collective impact, the stability and prosperity of the American economy as a whole.